SPACE

Nikalas Catlow

Tim Wesson

■SCHOLASTIC

Scholastic Children's Books,
Euston House,
24 Eversholt Street,
London NW1 1DB, UK

A division of Scholastic Ltd
London ~ New York ~ Toronto ~ Sydney ~ Auckland
Mexico City ~ New Delhi ~ Hong Kong

Editorial Director: Jill Sawyer
Editor: Catriona Clarke

Published in the UK by Scholastic Ltd, 2011

Text and illustrations by Nikalas Catlow and Tim Wesson
Text and illustrations © Nikalas Catlow and dogonarock (uk) Ltd, 2011

All rights reserved

ISBN 978 1407 11660 0

Printed and bound by Tien Wah Press Pte. Ltd, Singapore

The right of Nikalas Catlow and Tim Wesson to be identified as the authors and illustrators of this
work has been asserted by them in accordance with the Copyright, Designs and Patents Act, 1988.

This book is sold subject to the condition that it shall not, by way of trade or otherwise be lent,
resold, hired out, or otherwise circulated without the publisher's prior consent in any form of binding
or cover other than that in which it is published and without a similar condition, including this condition,
being imposed on a subsequent purchaser.

WARNING!

This Space book is seriously silly!

First CONTACT

What does this planet look like?

Silly space station

Finish the space station and make it silly!

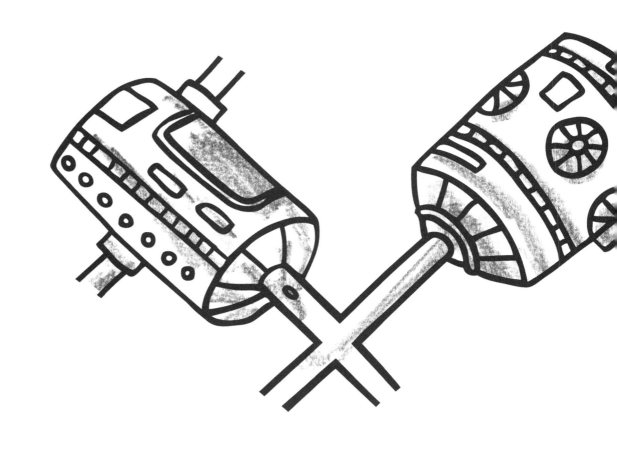

Colour and customize these familiar shapes into moons, planets and comets.

Planet footie

Lunar lemon

Marble meteor

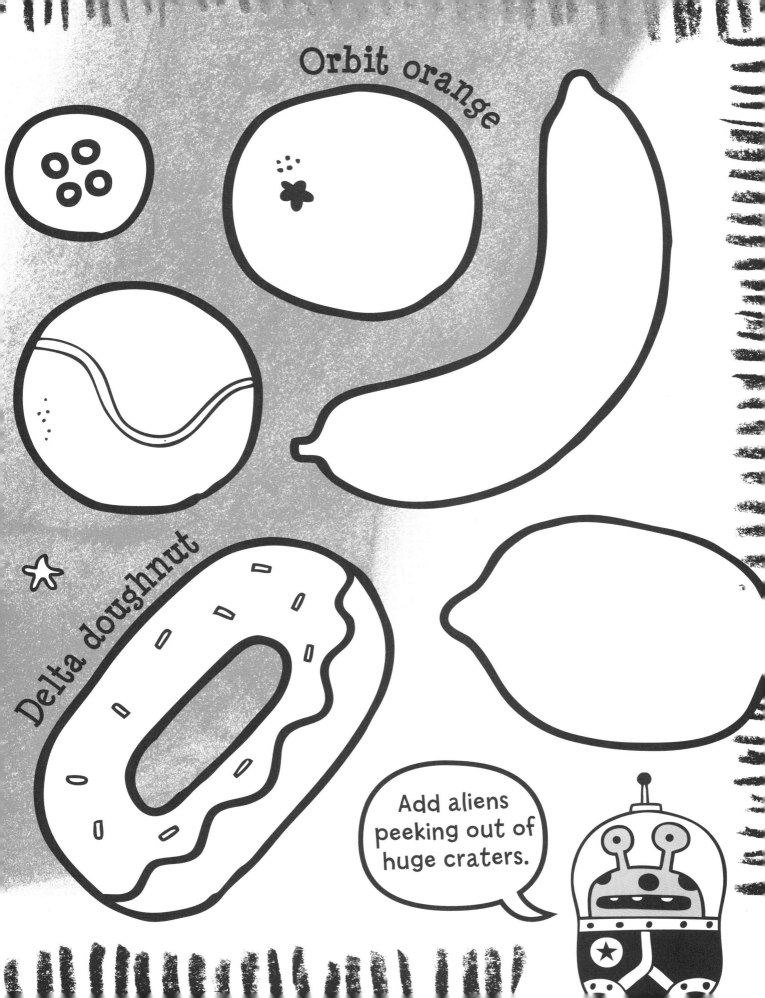

Robotic pants puzzle

Decode the alien messages!
(tip: A=Z, B=Y, C=X, and so on)

DV XLNV RM KZMGH

__ ____ __ _____

GZPV FH GL
BLFI OVZWVI

____ __ __
_____

____ _____

Create your own coded
message here.

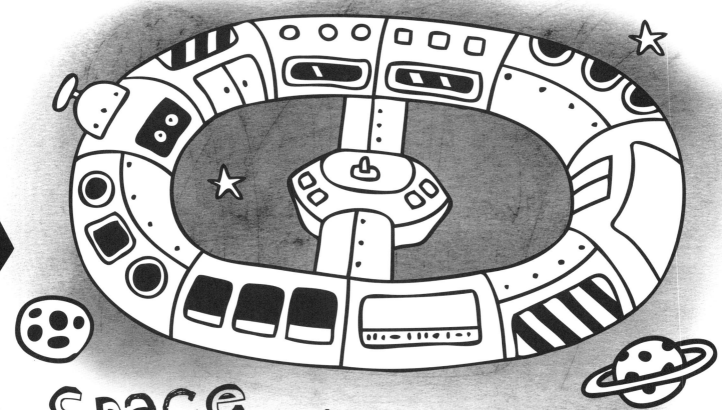

space station

Spot 5 differences.

Create your favourite alien of all time!

Hey!
I am an alien
Dweeb!

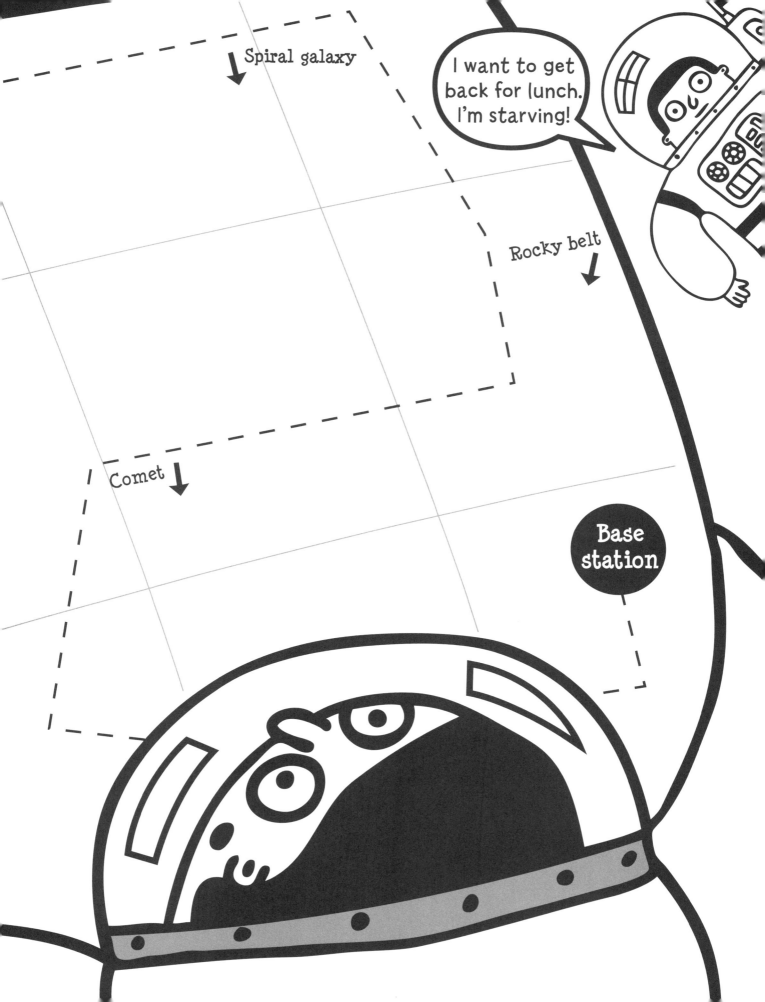

Captain Crater

The year was 2011 and Carl Crater was working in a factory packing frozen food into boxes. Suddenly he tripped and fell into a freezer and was frozen in time... Five hundred years later he has defrosted and is now the greatest galactic pilot in the solar system. Now Captain Crater and Astro Bunny are given their new assignment as intergalactic peacekeepers, assisting the Yergols on Planet X in their fight against the evil Oozebelch and his wicked plans to take over the galaxy.

Oozebelch is terrorizing the Yergols with terribly pongy cheese. The Yergols know what they like, and they don't like cheese. The Yergols are fond of fish though and like to bury their fish in a hole in the ground to let it fester.

And so Planet X and Oozebelch are locked in a galactic siege with the brave Yergols standing firm against him. Oozebelch orders his meany minions to fly low over Planet X and drop a ten-tonne cheese bomb on the Yergols. The angry Yergols fire the unwanted cheese back out into space with their giant catapult.

Next Oozebelch decides, 'It's time to unleash the mighty power of the Gyrating-Magnetic-Auto-Cheese-Sneeze machine.' And with that, the evil Oozebelch uncovers his secret plans for the deadly contraption and sets his meany minions the task of building it...

To be continued...

Now turn the book upside down and take the story quiz!

Quick quiz!

How many years was Captain Crater frozen for?

What is Oozebelch's evil plan?

What is the name of the inhabitants of Planet X?

Why doesn't Oozebelch's attack work?

What did Captain Crater fall into?

How did the Yergols get rid of the cheese that Oozebelch bombed them with?

What is the name of Oozebelch's henchmen?

Match these cosmic characters to their shadows on the next page.

oh no, here we go!

What else is being sucked into the black hole?

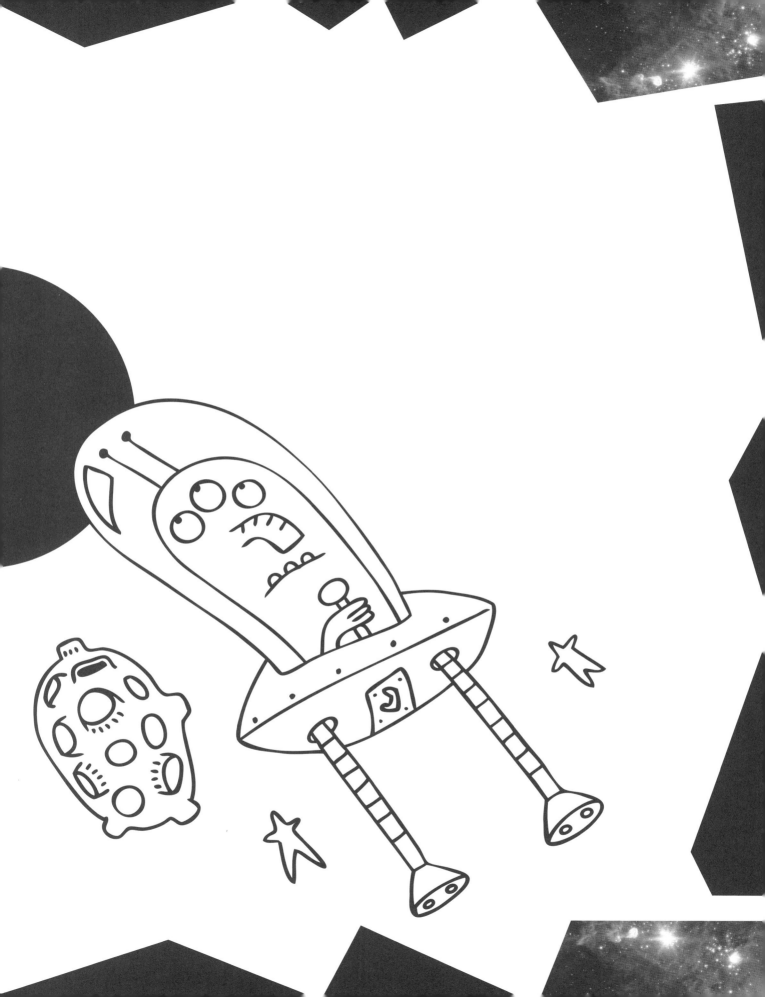

Captain Crater

1 Captain Crater, the greatest galactic pilot in the universe, is racing to stop the evil Oozebelch and his deadly Gyrating-Magnetic-Astro-Cheese-Sneeze machine.

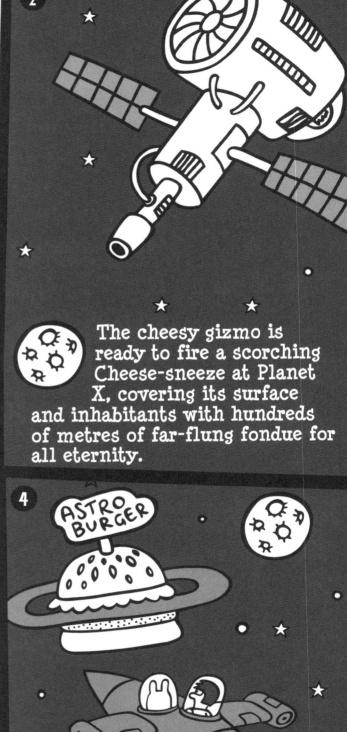

2 The cheesy gizmo is ready to fire a scorching Cheese-sneeze at Planet X, covering its surface and inhabitants with hundreds of metres of far-flung fondue for all eternity.

3 Power up the particle stirrer and light the vortex burners, my meany minion!

Aye, sir!

4 ASTRO BURGER

Meanwhile, Captain Crater decides to make a quick stop at a nearby fast-food space depot.

Pantastic CROSSWORD

Don't lose your pants in space — you'll never find them!

CLUES

DOWN
1. Humans have landed on it
3. The red planet in our solar system
4. The largest planet in our solar system
7. It shines brightly in the sky during the day

ACROSS
2. Similar to an asteroid, but with a long tail
5. The big planet with rings
6. They twinkle in the night sky

I wear rocket pants and fly around the Universe.

Asteroid hideout

Finish the scene.

Prepare to be zapped!

Would you rather

Draw an asteroid here.

Draw an alien ship here.

mission maze!

START

Can you make it to the black hole at the centre of the galaxy?

BLACK
HOLE!

Cosmic CROSSWORD

Down

1. You can get sucked into one
2. Edmond Halley named one
4. You fly through space in one
5. Saturn has one

Across

3. You re-enter it after returning to Earth
6. A rock that drifts through space
7. A round object big enough to have its own gravity
8. Where a spaceship takes off

FINISH
the ROCKET
for
launch

SPACE-oku

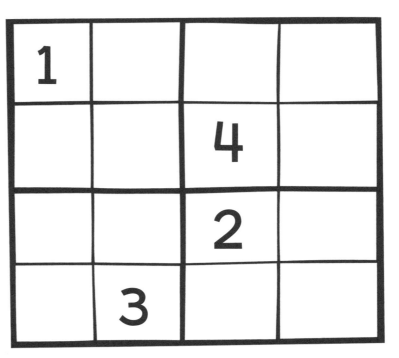

1			
		4	
		2	
	3		

Fill in the squares so that every row, column and 2x2 box contains the numbers 1, 2, 3 and 4.

Draw
Astro-
bot

We've started
you off with
his outline.

what's been zapped?

The Visitor

(YOU write the words!)

And now it's time for a...

Seriously Silly Space story

The evil Oozebelch has retreated in his escape pod to his space base Alpha Zooba to replenish his cheese stocks and to rebuild a bigger and better machine with which to defeat the Yergols. This time he will build a

_____.

Meanwhile, Captain Crater is on Planet X creating a secret plan called plan

_____ with the Yergols. 'We need as much fish as possible!' he explains to the rebel tribe.

Fill in the blanks with silly stuff!

Back at space base Alpha Zooba, a meany minion is peering at the radar screen. 'Sir, Captain Crater is approaching!'

'We have Alpha Zooba in our sights, Captain!' cries Astro Bunny, peering into his

_____.
But just then the space base defence system kicks in and lets loose with a torrent of _____ which whizz past the ship at lightning speed.

The captain's agile ship ducks and weaves to avoid the onslaught and when they're directly overhead, Captain Crater gives the order,
'_____.'
With that, the docking door opens and a hefty haul of stinking

_____ is ditched over Alpha Zooba, burying the evil Oozebelch and giving him a taste of his own stinky medicine . . . or fish, or

_____.

The End

Planet wordsearch
Can you find all eight planets in our solar system?

```
        V   A   N   O       X
    S   J   E   M       A   R   T
    A   J   P   N       P   S       O
E   T   B   S   V       U   N   E       S
A   U   R   A   N       U   S   N       F
R   R   N   E   P       T   U   N       E
T   N   J   U   P       I   T   E       R
H   I   M   E   R       C   U   R       y
Q   A   K   Z       B   E   D
U   R   F   N       E   S
    S   B   V       S   L
```

You don't need a telescope to find one of the planets!

Remember me

Look at this asteroid for about
a minute then turn the page.

NOW...

See if you can draw the picture on the previous page from memory.

No peeking at the previous page.

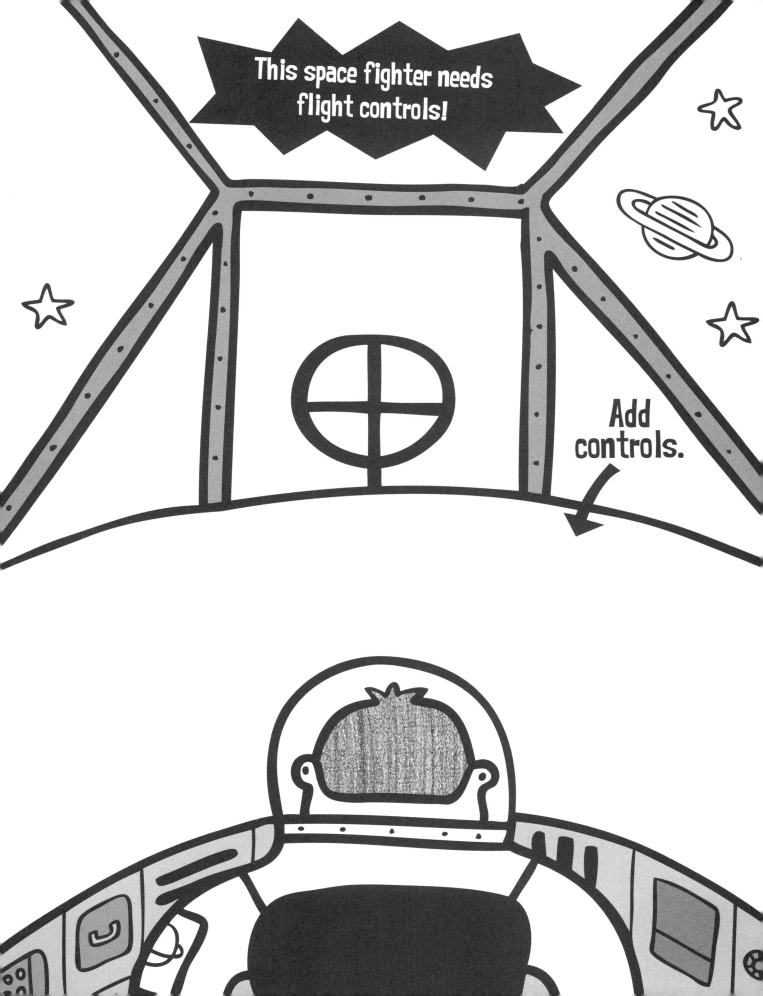

Action Andy

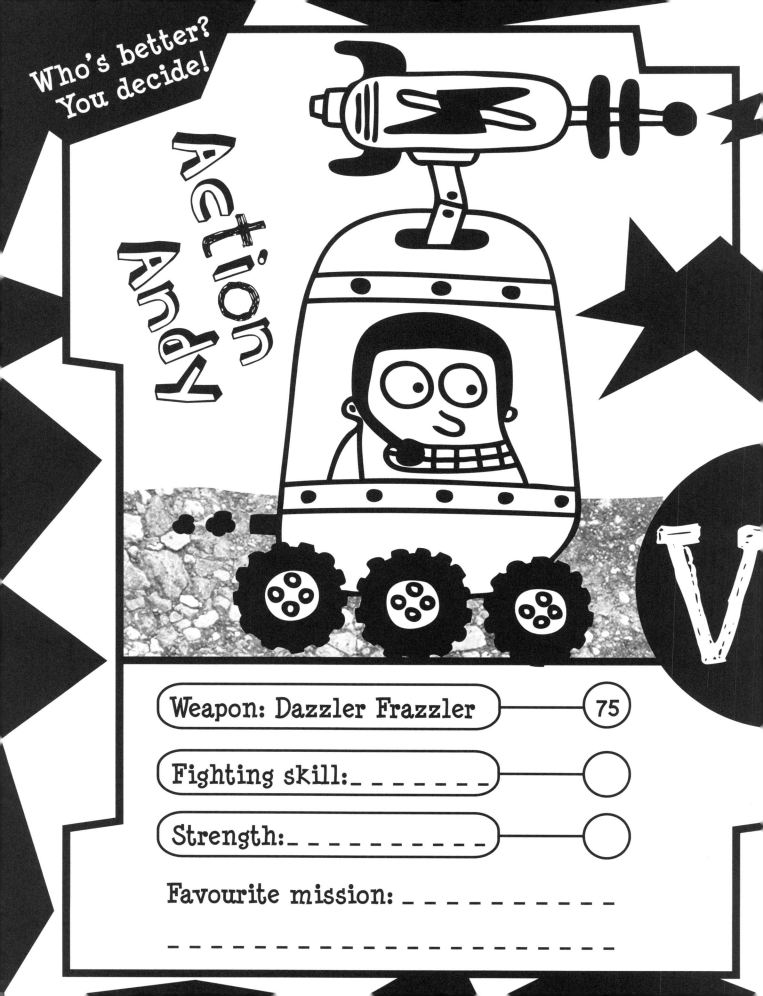

Weapon: Dazzler Frazzler — 75

Fighting skill:_ _ _ _ _ _ _ _ _

Strength:_ _ _ _ _ _ _ _ _ _ _

Favourite mission: _ _ _ _ _ _ _ _ _ _ _

_ _ _ _ _ _ _ _ _ _ _ _ _ _ _

Brian Blaster Bear

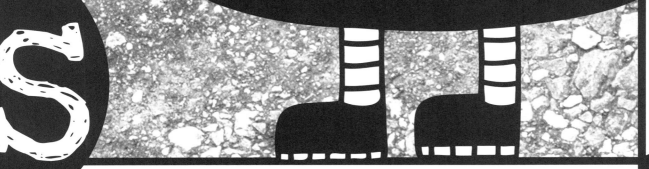

Weapon: Atomic bogey gun ———— 80

Fighting skill: _ _ _ _ _ _ _ _ _ ◯

Strength: _ _ _ _ _ _ _ _ _ _ _ _ ◯

Favourite mission: _ _ _ _ _ _ _ _ _ _

_ _ _ _ _ _ _ _ _ _ _ _ _ _ _ _ _ _

Moon man

Tim is a man on the moon. He looks after the moon base.

Hello!

I like maths.

He has a talented cat named Galaxy and a goldfish called Star to keep him company.

Today, Tim and Galaxy are taking the moon-rover out to collect rock samples.

The moon is covered with rock. They can't see anything interesting.

Back at the base Tim and Galaxy play a game of chess...

Check-mate!

...and turn off the artificial gravity at meal times.

Eventually it's time for bed. Goodnight, man on the moon.

Draw around your own hand and customize!

Create a background scene too.

COSMIC legS

Finish the bodies.

How to draw a rocket

...in four easy steps!

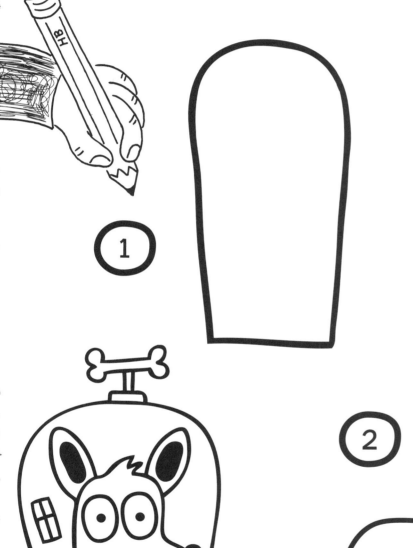

1

2

Draw someone peeking out of the porthole window.

3

4

Create your own rocket in the space above.

Would you rather

crash-land a bus on the moon...

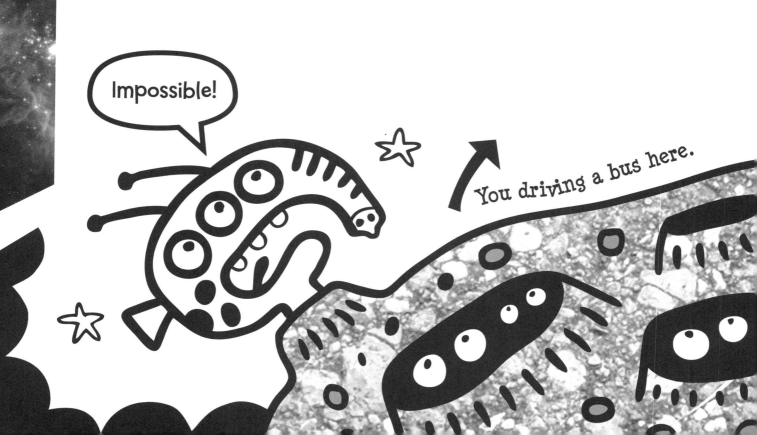

Continuous Scribble

Keep the line going and going...

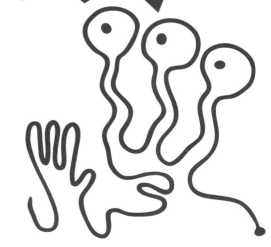

We need space legs

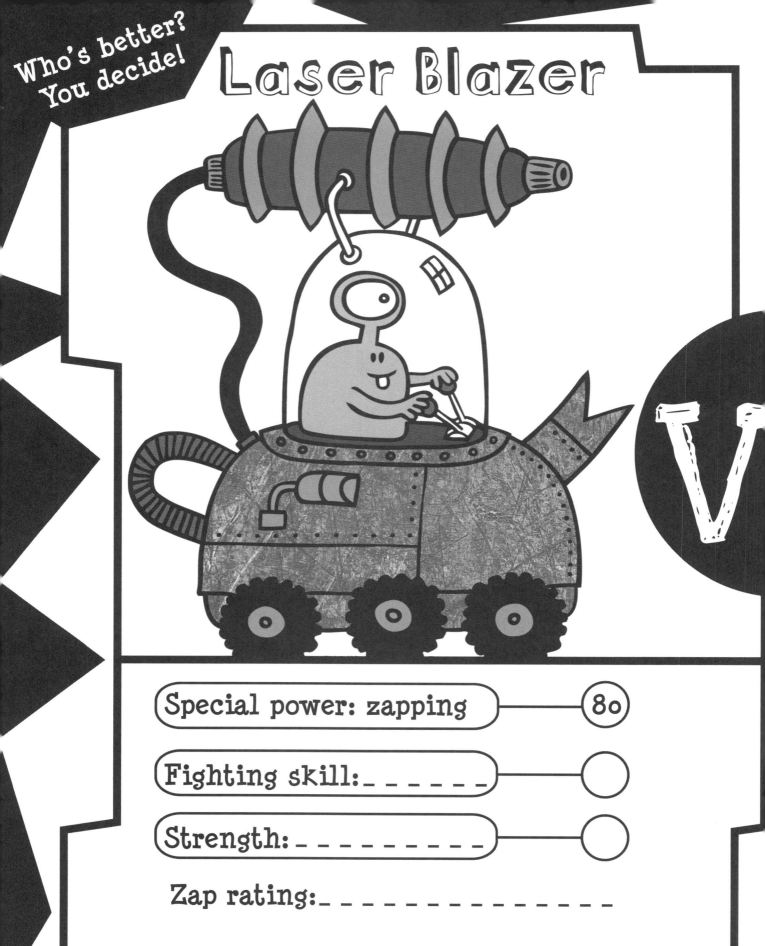

The BIG Sneeze

S

Special power: sneezing —————— (85)

Fighting skill:_ _ _ _ _ _ _ ()

Strength:_ _ _ _ _ _ _ _ _ ()

Snotty rating:_ _ _ _ _ _ _ _ _ _ _ _

_ _ _ _ _ _ _ _ _ _ _ _ _ _ _

Match them UP

...and finish them off!

finish

Spot the 5 differences!

Remember me

Look at this monster for about
a minute then turn the page.

NOW...
See if you can draw the picture on the previous page from memory.

No peeking!

Draw
a meany
minion

We've started
you off with
his outline.

Mars ATTACKS!

Finish the fleet of alien spaceships!

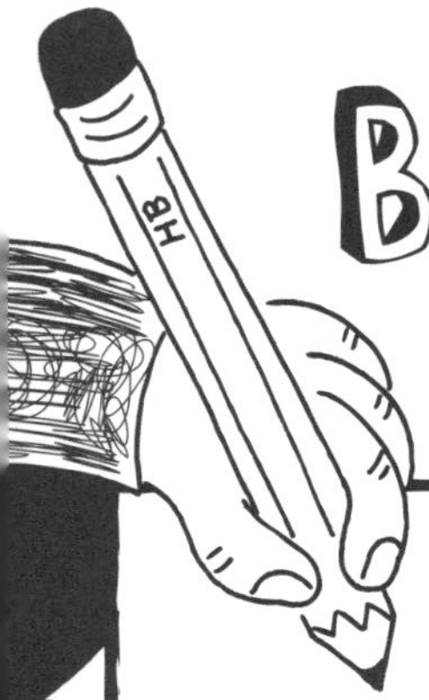

Boris Blobhead!
You draw the scenes!

1

Hello, I am an alien Dweeb. My name is Boris Blobhead.

2

This is my big bazooka ray gun, it has a ray warp button and a laser button.

3

Let me demonstrate on this Earth animal you call a cow.

4

The ray warp turns the cow inside out, causing it to moo loudly.

Show me all the silly action.

5

Switch to the laser and the cow is reduced to ash, unable to moo.

6

On our rocky planet we have no more mooing cows.

7

We live on a diet of chips and ash ... yum!

8

Farewell, Earthlings! I must fly back to Planet Dweeb for an ash lunch.

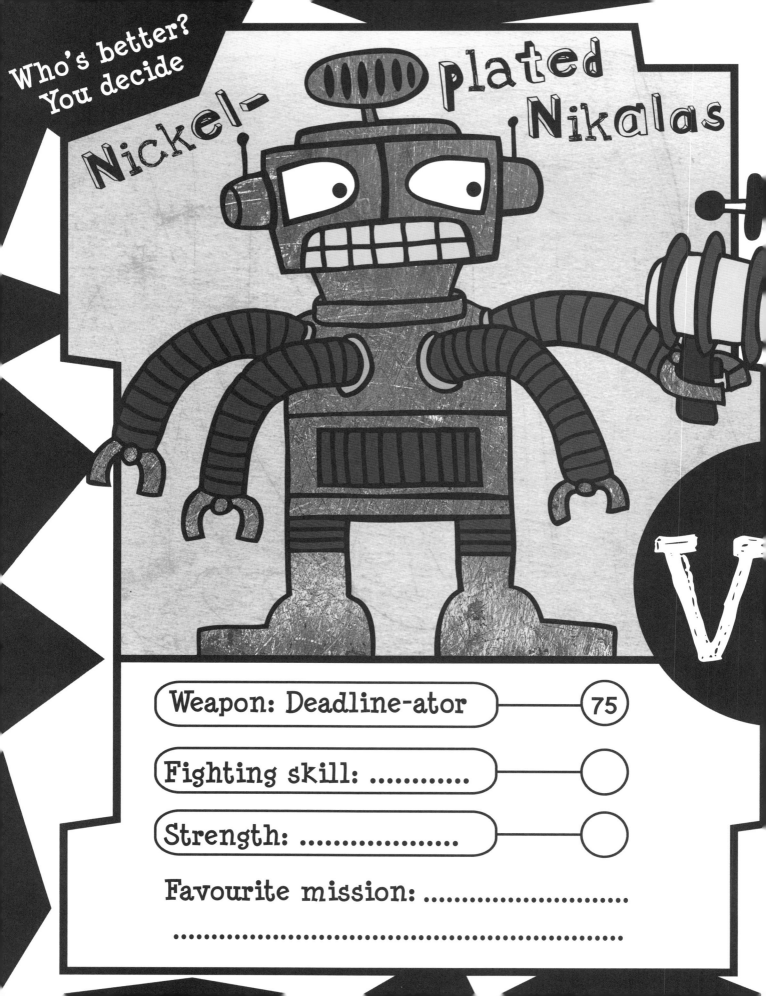

Draw your own

captain crater

...in **four** easy steps.

1

Follow the step-by-step instructions. It's easy!

2

3

Back down to Earth!

The Seriously Silly spaceship cleverly named 'The Impossible' is orbiting the Earth, 350 miles above the surface. Two astronauts are looking out the window.

'Hey my tummy is rumbling, let's fly back to Earth and have pepperoni pizza for lunch,' suggests Tim. 'Good idea,' says Nikalas. 'I'll start the ship's descent.'

'We've slowed down to 17,500 m.p.h. to enter the earth's atmosphere!' announces Nikalas. 'H-e-r-e w-e g-o, hold on to your helmet,' he adds. 'Woweeeee it's getting hot in here.' The temperature on the ship's surface is reaching 3,000oF. 'I'm switching to manual to guide us in,' announces Tim.

A few minutes later...
'We've slowed down to 200 m.p.h. Look I can see the seriously silly landing strip,' points Nikalas. 'Gently does it,' he adds. (Bump!)
'Hooray! We're down! Let's go and eat pizza!' claps Tim.

Quick quiz!

What is the name of the Seriously Silly spaceship?

How far up in orbit are they?

What pizza topping does Tim want?

How fast is the ship travelling when it enters the Earth's atmosphere?

What temperature does the ship's surface heat to?

What is the landing speed?

Do you want to be an astronaut?

Do you like pizza?

This is to certify that

Korbas

is now

SeriouSly Silly

about

SPACE

1,000 percent Seriously Silly.